ANIMAL KINGDOM POEMS

ANIMAL KINGDOM POEMS

Onye Kingsley

ATHENA PRESS
LONDON

ISBN 1 84401 326 X

First Published 2004 by
ATHENA PRESS
Queen's House, 2 Holly Road
Twickenham TW1 4EG
United Kingdom

Printed for Athena Press

Dedicated to animal lovers and animal charities world-wide

Contents

Preface

THESE POEMS WERE INSPIRED BY LOVE FOR NATURE

Y ou could imagine a world without dogs and puppies; a world without cats and kittens; a world without cattle, horses, pigeons, penguins, parrots and parakeets – the list is endless. And what a dull, empty and lonely world we all would be living in; our life spans would probably be touched by the loss.

As a boy of six, from a humble background in my rural, little, lonely village of Ihiala in Eastern Nigeria, even then I used to go hunting with my cousin in the nearby jungle without my parents' knowledge; even then I thought I was a superstar, the judge and jury over the animals world, slinging my cruel catapult, feeding it with little pebbles as I copied from my cousin who was older than me.

We never actually killed any big animal and only ended up coming home with small fish (fry) and crabs from our native flowing streams and brooks, which lie below a very dangerous precipice in our rural community. The large game was totally beyond our reach – we had no guns, and what magic would dare to provide us with one? So we learnt to content ourselves with what we had. Little did we know we were unfair to these poor creatures.

As the son of a disciplined senior police officer, in those days my dad was too busy to mind us; he was always being transferred. We had to follow him everywhere, and that meant new locations, new schools, new friends, new languages and new everything. At school I quickly made friends, keeping my love for animals in my heart until I met a friend of like mind. He had a cage full of rabbits – his father's business, of course. He fed them daily and later fell in love with them. I've always liked animals, to keep and protect them, and this was my opportunity to actually *own* one, and I wasn't prepared to miss it! I asked my friend to give me one. I was twelve by then, and so was my friend.

He knew I meant it, and he told his father who later asked me to pay half the money for one. I was overjoyed. Telling Mom would have been futile and a grave mistake, so I kept saving my pocket money and when some of Dad's friends visited they at times gave me some money, which I often saved, denying myself of goodies, just to achieve my goal.

One day I returned home with my rabbit, I had saved all the money and my friend ensured that I had a good deal – a pregnant rabbit, what a good friend!

I had no cage to keep it in, so I made do with my little room, away from Mom's prying eyes, Mom soon found out, she didn't do anything, but told me I was on my own as regards feeding it. We were a family of nine, and Mom's domestic budget was already overstretched and she had no space for my crazy adventure. That meant I couldn't afford to buy pellets, so I resorted to sharing my meals between me and my rabbit, and at times I supplemented our diet with vegetables and bush weeds. Who was I to complain? I loved what I was doing.

Dad too soon found out, but was indifferent. When my rabbit gave birth, to six siblings, I had to convert my kid sister's wooden baby cot into a rabbit cage, to contain my rabbit and her newly-born, hairless kids. Within just a few weeks all my rabbit siblings were all dead. I became depressed and ran to my friend to narrate my woeful tales. He asked me if I had touched the new siblings, and I said I had. He warned that I should never have touched the siblings because the mother often rejects them, stops giving them breast milk as soon as she perceives a strange odour on their bodies and they'll all soon die of starvation. That shocking revelation changed my life and perception of animals in general, so when next she gave birth, I never got so near to them; I simply watched from a distance and wished them well.

Before I knew it, I was already having more rabbits than I could ever think of. At that stage I kept giving them out as birthday presents to my friends, who promised they would look after them genuinely. I often paid surprise visits to their homes to ensure that they were all right.

As I ponder over the deplorable state of animals world-wide today, some thoughts creeps into my mind... *These animals are innocent, they survive on their own, they are their own doctors, their own nurses, their own police and military forces, their own lawyers and judges. They have no Citizens Advice bureau like us; they can't ask us for favours or help, and as a result of this many are now extinct or in danger. We owe them an obligation of care and protection – they are the beautiful part of our wonderful world.*

Hence ANIMAL KINGDOM POEMS; a token to animal charities world-wide, and you can be part of it.

Part One

The Poems

Pig

Rotund, my body looks; layers of fat: Creator's gift;
Saves me from the cold.
Very dirty, people say.
Not my fault, of course; one must feed, certainly,
From the gutters and rubbish-heaps of Master's leftovers.

Illness, do I hear you say? Forget it; like raindrops
On umbrellas: saves the farmer's dime; industrial revenues.
My nose ring is not for your wedding,
But food detection.

My love for dirt!
How I wish you could understand freedom,
Expressed on rubbish-heaps and in murky waters –
My ultimate pleasure.

Goat

With horns, though harmless,
With teeth I feed only on grasses.
'*Mmhmeh*,' that's how I cry.
Agile but stupid;
Purposeful but aimless.

Cud-chewing my greatest pastime,
Stubbornness, my lifestyle;
Bitter experience, easily forgotten.
Master of Ceremonies on Christmas Day.

Loved by all, but hated to bear my name,
Grow a beard to compete with men,
Knowing we aren't equals.
Just a place to chew my cud
In quiet, stupid cogitation…

Hen, Poultry

Imprisonment; my lot in life.
Wire-gauzed; my everlasting haven.
Countless eggs; never an offspring.
Have wings; can barely fly.
Feed on everything without teeth but beak.

Never stop pecking, saves nature; call to roast
Each passing day; a bonus in the hands of man,
Who could decide to sell or kill,
Anything he chooses, who cares?

Why not eat everything;
With man, one cannot be too sure.
Regular mesh and steady growth
Prepares one for the ultimate end.

Horse, Stallion

Strongly built; able-bodied; Trojan Horse.
Memories of those wars; those rustic times,
Dragged to battlefields; their will, not mine
Dragged to battlefields; their war, not mine.

Fully-loaded with saddles, mouth gagged, even metal-soles,
Robbed of every excuse to retreat.
What's more, rope in hands, painful side kicks,
Thorough lashing, makes one run like crazy.

Feeding? At their will, since mouth is gagged
With so-called metal, breathing itself, a special grace.
Fatigued? A non-issue;
Disobedience to orders a taboo.

Except you desire cracked back from unfriendly whips.
A million thanks to automobiles;
Without them I would have been long dead and buried…
I still handle little rough tasks like races,
But it's incomparable to rustic times.

Cat

Timid, ever sneaky, I vanish at unpleasant sounds,
Not always wanting to be seen, except at lunch times.
My love for exploits puts rats and birds on edge,
At the sound of *meow!*

Flee they must or face my wrath.
Like perfume, I detect their body scents. What next?
I dive to grab; and grab I must.

Selfish by nature,
I don't believe in sharing.
In a lonely corner I squat, to relish a victim.
Hairs, flesh and blood, even bones make nice delicacies.

I can be ruthless, if disturbed; some nasty spats
And claws could leave an intruder a sorry case.
As a pet you get the best of me,
The rest remains to be seen, is rather ignored.

Lion

S trolling the length and breadth of the jungle
In utter confidence with no care in the world,
Looking for one to devour, often succeeding.
Strong teeth; razor-like claws, a veritable edge.

Above all others.
Intermittent roar; all scamper for cover;
Never dare to wait and risk this single life.
King of the Jungle;
An African title none dare to contest.

Graceful and smooth strides are a total deceit;
My true self jumps out, at the sight of prey,
Who never say the last prayer in the sure
Face of death.

Pigeon

Innocuous creature, never hurting any,
Hovers in the sky like a helicopter, as free as the air.
Apple of every eye; anxious to be fed by all.
Wets its throat at the pools of Trafalgar Square;
Hundreds of like, entertain visitors.

Perching on their hands, heads and shoulders
With clean hearts, not killing hearts.
Never strays; alone, but with peers,
Unity is strength; their United Kingdom.

Tortoise

Appearance shows the manner.
A glance at you makes one quake with laughter,
Scurrying in pitiable strides;
Definitely gets to its proximity.
Always in hiding, like a snail, obviously.

A feeling of guilt and fear, not a saint.
Your crafted shell;
A wonderful haven that hides your bald head.
No one could bet a dime on your words.
Granny's folktales tell us who you are.

Cow

Multi-purpose creature; gladdens the hearts of man.
Your mountain-like structure calls for celebration.
Your meat serves the needs of men,
Your milk sustains our health; the milk of life.

Your bones and horns our industrial use;
Man cannot thank you enough, to heart.
Your strength ploughs our agricultural fields,
Which bring forth grasses that feed you.

Your dung our farmyard manure,
Your tough skin our leather shoes and bags;
Countless blessings and praise for you,
Cause for celebration.

Monkey

Master of treetops; acrobatic genius;
An easy escape mechanism, I suppose.
Man-like semblance, but a clear difference;
Movement on fours, rarely on twos.

Never found any art as beautiful as man,
Always desperate without much consideration for peers.
Your love for bananas knows no bounds;
A rib-cracker, you are, when clothed like man.

One wonders if any shoe could ever fit you,
And every watch an over-size to your tiny wrist.
Always squatting on the floor and treetops;
A far cry from decency. You can never be like man,
It doesn't matter how much you strive.

Hedgehog

H eavily guarded; heavenly armoured with
String-like strands; dangerous protrusions
Could pierce an invader at a moment's notice.

Ward off attacks by rolling self into ball,
Invader hurries away, glad to have escaped unhurt.
Coast clear, it uncoils itself, shuffles home to safety,
Thanking God for this precious gift.

Snake

Crawling rope, dreaded by all,
Charmers cannot even be too sure;
Like precious treasure,
Lying in the heat of the sunshine:
None dares move closer for a grab.

A single strike; Heaven-bound,
Without special grace to rescue.
Crafty enough to deceive first parents;
Genesis of enmity to mankind.
We bruise your head: you bruise our heels.

Genealogical game of wits.
Swallows; your feeding habits
Often land you in trouble:
At that feat, caution is thrown to winds
And attack an impossibility, since mouth is blocked.

Domination of man, you must accept;

At times one pities you,

when you shamelessly wriggle

Away in escape into your well-known hideout.

We ponder your mind's contraptions.

Dog

Ubiquitous pet; best of friends in household;
Shields master from dubious intruders.
Takes order, never speaks nor asks questions,
Could bark from dusk till dawn.

In protection of master,
My form of communication; my job.
Loyalty to master first law of nature,
Saying, 'Infallible Master, your wish is my command.'

Environmental sensitivity
My stock-in-trade, with smart nose.
Wagging of tail; welcome
Obeisance to the Lord of our home.

A pat on the head and gentle stroke at the back;
Master acknowledges receipt.
Bone-crushing my favourite pastime.
Got any for me to crush?

Elephant

Mighty Lord of the forest;
Hercules of the jungle.
Legs like tree-trunks,
Woe betide the grasses on which you tread!

Trunk – that elastic, multipurpose network –
Could accomplish impossible tasks in a flash.
Ears like banana leaves at our farm yard
Could sift news.

How this stomach gets filled up is
An earthly miracle.
Litres of water that fill this tract,
News of our time.

Tusks; a sweet-bitter gift of nature,
A treasure they are, but life threatening
To him when poachers lurk next door,
Waiting to have them by hook or by crook.

Giraffe

Artistic masterpiece, your body design,
A fur that leaves a designer green with envy.
Your long, stretched neck makes a spy
Green with envy.

From here you see everywhere,
Like gossips acquainted with goings on
From every nook and cranny.
Soft leaves you feed on, with your tiny teeth,
Harboured in your little head.

One never stops to ponder the long, tortuous
Journey of those leaves from mouth,
Through that awful neck to your stomach.
A long trek indeed!

Harmless as you are, those four legs are
Olympic gold standard;
How you coordinate those members
Is an additional wonder of the world.

Ostrich

Queen of birds, of types and times,
  Your enormous physique, a wonder to many.
Flight for you is an after-thought;
Little wonder you take it out on races,
Can run endless miles – what a might!

Eggs bigger than any lower likes could afford;
Yet so protective.
Naked from neck to head,
Vulture-like, is it?
Those strong beaks; instruments of all times.

Burying head in sand;
What a way to dodge enemies, what a way to hide!
What becomes the fate of other members?
Possibly not important enough.
Oh, incomprehensible folly/wisdom, you know better!

Parrot

Sickle-like beak; word-leaker,
Ever loquacious, open secrets.
Who cares! Friend of the Master, conversational partner?
Talking from the cage
A regular pastime; stream of visitors.

Stream of messages, each well recorded
Not wanting to mingle words,
Even the Master's secret; cat's out of the bag!
Little wonder Master is always
Cautious each time you are around,
Knowing you could spill the beans.

Bull vs. Fighter

R ed cloth to him a taboo;
  A sight of any means a troubled spot.
Heavily built, fierce horns to match.
Costumed; a perfect cowboy.

Ultimate goal; bullfighting.
Love for martyrdom a propelling force.
Betwixt life and death game of double wits,
Heavens save the cowboy!

Bull's back the next line
Tantrum, objections, charges the bull.
Till back is free, Heaven save the fighter
Hat flung metres away,

Himself half on the bull, half in air,
Fate in quandary.
Either must taste the bitter pill
Of death; martyrdom.
Fate decides.

Camel

A rabian car; Lord of the desert,
Could journey days on end, on grassless lands,
waterless lands,
Wide geographical spread, with heaven and earth.
Endurance of thirst, incomparable.

Countless luggage, other paraphernalia
A nip in the bud.
Must go on knees for Master to climb aback.
Endurance of unfriendly weather; kudos to your health.

Grizzly Bear

L and and sea, a perfect haven rain or shine.
 Ever-smiling, dog-like face; save for stature.
Formidable strength; a destructive might,
Claw-infested toes; some dare-devils.

Fur a standing ovation for designers,
who engage it in countless styles for fans.
How marketable you are!
Those fishes and leaves you feed on
Your good complements, so ride on.

Scorpion

S mooth on the surface; poison at the tail,
A sting; bucketful of tears.
Know no bounds: adults, youths,
Even six-legged; everyone's a suspect.
Come not near and nurse no regrets.

Know no play; avoided by all –
Will attack even in your own domain, your own territory.
Always on the offensive,
Has no friends. Sting on prey spells doom.
None could stand to argue or negotiate,
With eyes full of tears.

At times; tantrums; unable to bear the sting.
Babies on back, always, learning this warfare.
Soon masters of their own independence.
They'll say, 'What a beautiful tail I have.'

Cockroach

B eneath your clothes; in wardrobes,
Your cupboards, hidden corners of your place;
There I'll be, waiting for you,
With a packet of surprises at my disposal.

Could turn your Christmas wears into rags in seconds.
Your wedding suit; my suit;
Your shoe I even tried on my feet.
Never can tell; it may be my size.

I wore them, though, out of your sight.
'Cos I know you'd complain,
Or possibly threaten dear life.
Fast shifting base from your stupid kitchen
And toilet to sitting.

Room, our room.
Your TV, radio sets, even car,
I'll soon lay hands on.
Never think I'm scared of those
Rantings of yours.

Spider

At the very corners of your wall
I'll ever be present; those spectacular joints.
How I enjoy those spots beyond your imagination.

My complex mansions; ideal home,
Sheltered by your roof.
I never travel; except occasional migration in austere times.
I have the perfect home that feeds its owner;
Paradise on earth.

Only wait to devour captives, without much hassle.
My building instrument a wonder to many;
My complex engineering mechanisms a near miracle:
My little brain.
Your so-called modern computer to me is child's play.

Housefly

A bloody wanderer, you may call me,
Coming around to say 'Hi' now becomes a bad idea,
does it?
Never mind my hand-washing,
Only helping to ensure a prayer before your meal
Knowing you could forget.

Perching everywhere, friendly to all,
Never harbour grudges, could transmit diseases.
Do I hear, you say? Like a dove, my harmlessness, I swear!
Those scientific statements you should forget.

Giving a dog a bad name, to hang it;
A human device.
Little wonder I'm often chased around
With brooms and insecticides,
Soon going to get immune to those.

But why such cruelty to a dear friend,
Who often calls to say 'Hi'?
A friend who prays and wets your food
For your blessed consumption?

I'll have a re-think about this
One-sided friendship, that is fast turning
One into a social nuisance,
Like a handshake going beyond the wrist...

Mosquito

Coward of the night; naughty vampire
Never allows a moment's sleep, after
A day's drill. Steals in like a thief in the night,
Waiting to rob the unwary of costly blood.

Coward, do I hear you say?
Don't you observe the noise
I make right to your hearing?
After all, it's only a drop
Here and there, not much anyway.
I must confess that you have some honey
Right there, which makes me risk this single life.

Your occasional slaps leaves one at the mercy of
Our Lord. And each time you succeed, you feel so
Delighted that you switch on your stupid
Light to behold my crushed body, smearing
Your own blood on yourself what a shame!

At times you spray those silly chemicals,

Even smokes, when you really want to be cruel.

All in desperate ploy: to stop me, and stop Nature's works.

You lock-up everywhere.

Hoping I've been locked out,

Not knowing I'm squatting at your curtains,

Warming-up for tonight!

Butterfly

So beautiful; so graceful; so lovely,
Nature must have worked on you on the Sabbath.
Nothing else could better explain
Such flawlessness in your creation.

Those flowers will ever be grateful for your care.
Little wonder they produce
Those tasty juices – their widows – mites.
Your multiple colours, a sight to behold.

A beautiful dancer, you are; perching on
Those flowers with utmost care,
Like a mother tendering her newly-born baby.

Bee

Like gold, my complexion; a veritable workman,
Hours on end in my field.
That golden juice; for my kith and kin,
The juice of life.

Workman at his tools; lazy man in his idleness,
You've cost me a lot; all my savings robbed overnight.
Smoking me out of my kingdom, kith and kin;
Most dead; few survived.

What cruelty! Can't you fashion a substitute
For your rabid cravings for the fruits of my toil?
Unable to stop you;
Like hell I had to sting you silly.

A defence mechanism that never works for long,
For I always end up with my colleagues
In the graveyard,
Leaving my golden honey to sustain your cruel life.

Ant vs. Grasshopper

'Ha, ha! You tiny creature,
Who never allows a minute's rest,
You'll soon die, may not live
To taste your stores.'

'Your curse like rain on an umbrella;
Better be late than be the late, the wise say.'
'Too busy to store in the midst of plenty,
No glutton could finish all that in years to come.'

'Friend, don't learn the hard way;
Famine in the offing, make haste while the sun shines.'
'Possibly you intend to grow to my stature, pint-sized?
That could make you the comic of the century, you know.'

'Don't insult me, after all, all in your head is a vacuum.
Wait and see whose laugh comes last.
What an awful winter, got no job
Other than to freeze food and vegetables.'

'Quite hungry, need to act fast lest one dies,

Yeah, a bright idea; got to visit Ant!

A friend in need is a friend indeed,

Some foodstuff from him will do.'

Knock, knock! 'This time of the night? Who is it?'

'Just open-up, freezing to death!'

'Hopper, is that you?' 'Who else if not me?

I'm starving to death, some grains will do.'

'Pal, whose laugh comes last?'

'Yours of course, some grains please!'

'Can't afford to part with a seed,

Never had you in mind during storage. Goodnight!'

Snail

B ound of flesh with house to drag,
Dragging all day till life expires.
What a fate to behold, amid life's wonders.

Liquids abound in no small measure,
To lubricate body-shell contact,
Could form a cyst when times are hard.

Dwell on last storage within the enclosure,
What a wonderful life to live?
What a mystery; what a burden?

Crab

By the seashore and river banks my dwelling place,
Soft grounds I drill to make holes that accommodate me,
Moisture and water droplets in the hole matter not.
Six legged; with scissor-like claws,
Ever ready to attack at the slightest provocation.
Sideward movement as I scuttle to my hole to rest my head.

My head that never exists,
'Cos I'm built-up like an armoured tank,
With dot-like eyes that pick you out like a satellite
Wherever you are, friend or foe.

My chest, my natural bag, my bank account;
There I safely keep my things – kids and valuables –
Away from your wicked gaze and sticky fingers.
Don't blame me, though!

Praying Mantis

Like a boxer, your posture;
Angled hands, with countless pins
Set to attack, and often do.

Hind legs, a worthy support,
Giving strength to your frame.
One often wonders how you dare all, in desperate bouts.

Your leaf-like colour puts one in a quandary,
As you freely mix in among those greens,
Quietly escaping the counter-challenge you've initiated.

Leopard

Dark patches all over your skin in countless spots,
Fellow animals your daily bread.
Often stoop to pounce on the unwary,
A surprise visit that leads to their demise.

Bag of tricks as you launch attacks on prey,
Your fellows in the kingdom.
Countless rainstorms have often tried,
Ceaselessly, though, to rub off your spots to no avail.

How you wish you had wings to fly!
Birds' lives could be endangered,
Since no place on land is sacred.
Heard you even compete with fish in the waters –
Could that be true?

Millipede

L iving train with tiny coaches
Of circular segments as body,
Tiny millions that pass as legs, hence your name,
All moving in waves and waves.

Passing through thick and thin;
Smooth and rough terrain, destination unknown.
Ever shining, ever clean,
But never a bath.

The marvel of nature;
Legs as stickers on the walls,
Crawl on leaves and trees,
Even the most terrible terrain an easy glide.

Coils at the touch of the enemy,
Seeps a solemn thought...
'Let them think I'm dead and leave me alone,'
Nature's unspoken thoughts.

Chameleon

Multi-coloured living wonder of ancient days,
Dragged to the present.
Struggling to walk, like an old man
With his walking stick.

How far can you trek in this manner?
Heaven knows!
Little wonder you often change colour
To suit wherever you are and deceive us.

One wonders at your oath with Mother Nature,
Who endowed you with long, curly tongue
That spells doom to prey,

And quickens your appetite as you flick it
To the detriment of innocent prey,
Who often mistake you for objects
As you perch on a twig, and are doomed.

Bat

Funny looks, my looks,
Strange one, you may say.
Ratty heads you can see, but how does one explain?

My wings like umbrellas;
A far cry from birds' –
I couldn't live in a nest like them.

My fur-covered skin
A far cry from feathers,
Perching on twigs.

My other miracles: hanging upside down
In acrobatic display of ancient China.
Dusk and dawn; my normal days;
Perfect light in caves where I dwell.

Cricket

S ilent in the day; vibrant at night,
Shrill upon shrill
As if night has just broken into daylight,
Not caring whose ox is gored.

With noise that pierces the eardrums;
Disorganising the rational thought of men.
'What's it all about?'
One wonders aloud.

'Communication, of course,'
Replies a silent voice,
'With meanings deeply buried in the thickness of the
Blackness of the darkness of the midnight.'

Dolphin

Tropical waters; temperate regions
Of the Atlantic waters of this world,
There I can be found.
Shallow, warm, inshore waters my proper haven;
Polar Regions, my taboo.

Sounds emitted via my nasal sac,
My communication form.
As I chat along with mates and moles –
Vile and villainous –
In my unpredictable life at sea.

My tail, my throttle that powers me
Through the waters to safety
As I hate surprises by predators,
Vile and villainous, who often lurk in the dark,
Waiting to gamble with my single life
That has no duplicate.
Like thunder from hell I shoot away to safety,
As every new day now becomes a bonus in my life.

At sea, life's battle is either won or lost;

There are no midways in the animal kingdom.

At times I get too close to humans,

But often get betrayed,

Though that won't stop me as I see them

As an integral part of our beautiful world.

They effect changes as they ride me like a horse,

Through the high seas of this world when at play;

As I teach them how to swim; my playmates.

Penguin

Antarctica's icy coastline region of this planet;
My haven, my paradise on earth with those icy waters.
Frozen, floating flakes flowing freely,
Freezing all that comes its way. My home away from home.

Tapering tube-shaped body;
My resistance to cold that could be the end of you.
Yellowish orange-like streak; my black bill that feeds me
And keeps me at peace or war,
Whichever way the pendulum swings, friend or foe.

Layers of body fat; dense, insulating plumage,
My safe haven from the frigid cold of my world,
Never could ask nature for more.

My webbed feet, my rudders like a boat's in the waters,
But on land I'm rubbish and can only manage an awkward
waddle.
When tired, I could toboggan on my stomach,
Using my wings to push along.
A hard life, you may think, but it's my fun.

Faithfulness in relationships our hallmark,

With unique call signals that track down mates and loved ones.

Feeding on fish and krill, at times squid.

As an excellent swimmer, I dive like thunder

Into the astounding depth of the seas

Like a rocket fired into the heavens;

Nature's gift, none dares to challenge.

Zebra

Lovely stripes of black and white,
My nature's pride and patterns.
That makes me a target for friends and foe;
As they gets closer, their eyes you can see,
But hearts you can't.

This leaves me at sea with only the sure way of escape
My intuition; my perception; my legs; my strength.
Life in the wild;
Horror as predators make the weak their mincemeat,
Robbing us of our dear life in the broad daylight,
Not to mention the awe of the nights.

The million-pound question remains unanswered:
Man could build our parks; Man could build our zoos;
Man could build our preservation centres,
But who can save us from ourselves, in our animal kingdom,
Where might is always right?

Panda

B amboo-leaved forest of south-west China's fragmented
mountains;
There lies my palace with no care in the world.
Bamboo leaves my saviour from the wicked pangs of hunger,
As I chew away, drowning my sorrows to stay afloat.

My colour blend, my gift from nature to hide away
From the vile and villainous;
The predators that seek my precious life to take.
My anal glands secure my territory
With their pungent secretions that give clear signals
To intruders, to mind their business and keep off.

My paw-pads, infested with mighty claws;
Those are my arsenal as I do battle in the wild,
Where the only language that ever makes sense
Is the survival of the fittest, where might becomes right,
Not minding whose ox is gored.

Skunk

My life in the wild; a long story that fires your imagination.
I often mind my business as I run my daily life,
Sorting out my food, shelter and family, if I have one.

My love of treetops; my good news; my fortress
As enemies sneak about searching for my single life,
For them to take or leave me a sorry case with regrets
If I manage to escape, or worse still;
As a carcass for others to feast on.

No way! Attack, they say, is the best form of defence
As I sport my white stripe; my regular badge to warn you off
The vile, villains and predators of my world,
My last warnings before I bath you with my foul-smelling liquid.

This could spell your doom,
Make you an outcast among mates and family,
Because they won't stand how horribly you'll stink,
As I wash you dirty with my priceless fouling gift, my arsenal.

Rhinoceros

Like a hook, the stump on my nose,
Thick-skinned, sturdy legs; all I could get from nature.
Life in the wild; my lot in life.
Austere times, egrets perch on my back, picking up ticks,
The parasites that suck my blood without paying a dime.

Later they do in the egret's tummy as a meal subsidy, of course,
Complimenting her desired nutrients.
Nature's intricate food-chain,
A web that links all living that have breath
And none are spared the agony and grief.

My territory; a no-go area; else it's fight to finish –
Winner takes all and wears the crown,
The crown of glory that makes the bearer
A sure target for all contenders;

The more vulnerable in this complex world

Of challenge and counter-challenge.

Better enjoy it now whilst it lasts,

For tomorrow is not promised to anyone.

Whale

Like a mansion in the wild, wide world's high seas;
So I'm bobbling with life and spewing waters
From the oceans of this globe.
A celebrity, when compared to others.

At the sight of me others scampers to safety,
Knowing they could be swallowed hook, line and sinker
In one single gulp and without a trace.

Inside of me is like a stadium, a conference hall,
Where no meeting is ever held except
Digestion of swallowed objects.

A veritable source, I am, of oil;
When occasion demands and the sick are healed using it:
My token of appreciation for nature's goodness,
Making me the king of the dead, dark depth off shore's high
seas.

As Jonah is safely kept for three days and nights,
Our biblical legend says it all.

Octopus

Ten legged, they call me, with mighty eyes to match.
None can escape me; with all eight I'll go for you,
Peace or war, any way the pendulum swings.
I squirt black ink to deceive enemies and hide myself,
When the going gets tough.

Who wants to die young? Whatever for?
Beneath my arms are suction cups,
Holding onto anything that runs into me,
Friend or foe.
Boneless wonder, that I am very flexible;
Little wonder I bend like Beckham!

Kangaroo

Wonderful, they call me,
Marsupial, the secondment.
Carrying my joey in my pouch,
My trademark.

Australian pride,
Prancing about on two whilst having four,
The strength of my hind legs enough to weather any storm,
While the fore help with domestics.

Australian jungles; my paradise on earth.
Sweet, sweet, happy, humble home.
Your bedtime; my fun-time, as I skip about in search of
Daily bread for self and siblings.

At times the enemy lurks in the dark
To cut off this single life.
The signals from my alarmed, dog-like head
Spurn my hinds into athletic feats that beat an
Olympic gold medallist, leaving him green with envy.

As I skip with all I've got, kith and kin,

To a serene, secluded, solitary safety,

Where I can now sleep with my two eyes closed.

Fox

Dog-like features, but poles apart;
Cruelty marks the difference.
A bloody nuisance, all agreed.
Selfish from birth; never cares whose ox is gored.

My lot in life.
'With a friend like you, who needs an enemy?' chorused the
chicken.
As you often lay ambush on their single life,
With your cruel teeth that lack mercy.

Unwelcome visitor at every home,
'Cos of the darkness in your heart
And mischief at every breath that you take.

Only few could have mercy on you.
As hunters chase you out of planet earth
With dogs, guns, clubs and cudgels,
To seal your doom and save the chicks, the farmers' pride.

Rabbit

Rich grasslands, with burrows hidden away and out of sight;
My lovely place. Grazing in groups with ears alert,
Watching out for safety, the gimmick of survival.

Strong and folded hind-legs, my Olympic sprints
As I let loose my speed
When life is at risk, throwing myself in the air as I hop
To the safety of my home; my lovely burrow.
There I kept my all in all, kith and kin.

In our world, shutting your eyes is a taboo,
'Cos you'll never know; enemies could strike.
The reason nature endowed us with large ones –
I mean, my eyes.

Part Two

Explanation of the Poems

Pig

The poet applauds the animal's natural endowments and sees its dirtiness-yet-healthiness as a blessing to its owner, who will save his money instead of paying exorbitant medical bills. It is expected that a pig will often be sick because of the degree of dirt it accommodates.

Goat

The poet extols the stupid nature of the goat and sees it as harmless as ever and nurses no grudge against any, even when it has been slaughtered for ceremonies. Its stubborn and often forgetful nature is well celebrated. Most people like goat meat, but none ever like to be called a goat.

Hen, Poultry

Hen is an examination of the fate of poultry and the ordeals they go through, those countless hours of caged waiting, laying eggs or being sold to be slaughtered for feasts. They loathe their fate at the hands of man.

Horse, Stallion

This poem celebrates the awful fate of horses during the medieval period, when there were no armoured tanks or automobiles, jetfighters or warship, and horses were extensively used for all these tough tasks, not of their own will.

Cat

Hails the nature of cats with close reference to their relationships with rats, mice and even human begins. The cat's queer nature is well celebrated.

Lion

Celebrates the self-confidence and natural endowment of the African lion; the panic and pandemonium often caused by its roar in the jungle and its attacks on prey.

Pigeon

Lauds the innocence of the pigeon and its friendly relationship with human beings, especially visitors at parks, who often long to feed it from their palms.

Tortoise

A celebration of the hidden and crafty nature of the tortoise. Its patched-up body makes it an object of ridicule, and it often appears in folklore as a crook.

Cow

Celebrates the natural gifts of cows: the supply of milk, our source of protein, beef; their hides; even their bones and horns can be used in manufacturing industries.

Monkey

This poem celebrates the ridiculous monkey as a poor imitation of man, noting its greed, its love for bananas, its tree-climbing antics and how it looks when dressed like man.

Hedgehog

Praises the natural defensive gifts Mother Nature has bestowed upon the hedgehog as it shields its body with protective components, helping it to escape from enemies. The poem evokes a mental picture of how the hedgehog rolls itself into a ball to escape attack.

Snake

Celebrates the natural endowment of the snake and comments upon the genesis of its enmity towards mankind and its feeding habits. Where the snake regards its place in the natural scheme of things and the age-old issue of dominion are all well celebrated.

Dog

An exploration of the mutual relationship between dog and man and a dog's protective instincts towards man, who it sees as Master all the time. The sensitive nose of the dog is also celebrated. Finally, the mutual understanding that exists between dog and man in matters of greetings, salutation and acknowledgement is revealed.

Elephant

Exalts the mighty nature of the elephant as the largest animal in the jungle. Celebrates its trunk for all the work it does for the elephant. The poet sees its tusks as a 'sweet-bitter gift of nature': sweet in the sense that they help the elephant in attack and defence when in trouble and bitter because poachers kill elephants unreasonably in a bid to get their tusks, thus reducing their numbers drastically.

Giraffe

This poem applauds the giraffe's natural patterns and its body design as people admire it. The poet talks about the length of its neck, comparing it with other spies. The poet further celebrates the height and body coordination of the giraffe.

Ostrich

Celebrates the nature of the ostrich as the biggest of all birds. It cannot fly but can run very fast should the need arise. The poet is amazed by the fact that the ostrich buries its head in the sand and sees it as a funny way to hide from enemies. '*Oh, incomprehensible folly/wisdom*': foolish because everybody can see him yet he claims to be hiding, and wisdom because to the ostrich himself it's the height of intelligence.

Parrot

Exalts the loquaciousness of the parrot and explores what endears it to man and what limits our admiration.

Bull vs. Fighter

Applauds the danger bedevilling the act of bullfighting. The poet explains the aim of the bullfighter and what his success hinges upon.

Camel

The poet sees the camel as an obedient beast of burden who reveres its owner. He celebrates the patience and the endless endurance of camels in the dessert during inclement weather.

Grizzly Bear

Glorifies the strength and the might of the bear and expresses the usefulness of its fur to fashion designers.

Scorpion

A celebration of the poisonous nature of the scorpion, which stings anyone at will; even the strongest man will be in tears at its sting. The poet further mentions how the scorpion carries its young on its back and teaches them the wicked art of attack with the use of the deadly tail.

Cockroach

The poet examines the various activities of cockroaches in our homes; in the kitchen, wardrobes, even in the sitting room, doing damage to our properties.

Spider

The poet celebrates the activities of the spider and its cobwebs in the corners of our homes, examining how it entangles its prey. The spider boasts of its intelligence and tact, despising man's computer age.

Housefly

The poet applauds the insect's activities in relation to man's loathsomeness of it. It mentions that man uses insecticides and various modes of pest control on it, and this, it claims, is an act of wickedness to a dear friend who loves man dearly.

Mosquito

The poet celebrates the nefarious activities of mosquitoes and how they enter one's place of abode and suck precious blood, transmitting diseases to the detriment of man.

Butterfly

The poet showers praises on the beautiful nature of the butterfly, saying that nature probably waited for the Sabbath day (the last day of the week) to spend overtime in beautifying her. He further mentions that flowers must be very grateful for the way she attends to them – like a mother tending her newly-born baby.

Bee

The workaholic nature of the bee is brought to light by emphasis from the poet. He ensures that he provides enough honey for his family (kith and kin) only to be robbed in a broad daylight by lazy humans who smoke him and his family out of their home and steal their precious food (honey). He often wonders why man cannot put his hands together and work harder to achieve whatever he needs. In annoyance, the bee often stings man but only ends up dead, leaving them to enjoy the hard-earned fruits of his labour.

Ant vs. Grasshopper

A conversation between two great friends – the ant and grasshopper, with reference to the proverb 'make haste while the sun shines and never leave it too late.' The message here is don't wait for success – *go for it!*

Ant is wiser than the grasshopper because he took the time to store enough food in his home before the difficult season of winter, an austere time, while his friend grasshopper was busy gallivanting around, only to face the hard times unprepared for the shock that awaits him.

Snail

The poet explains why the snail drags her shell everywhere she goes – she's got a house to drag. He further mentions the function of the bodily fluids of the snail; how it helps her to lubricate shell/body contact, how she forms cysts to store her food and protect herself from dying of hunger during famine.

Crab

The poet describes the natural habitat of the crab. He mentions his defence mechanism – his large claws, his sideward movement, and his seemingly headless body: "*Cos I'm built-up like an armoured tank*'. He further mentions the sharpness of her eyes – like a satellite. Her pouch-like chest is her storage facility.

Praying Mantis

The attacking posture of the praying mantis is celebrated by the poet; how she stands up to her enemy, supporting herself with her legs. He points out that most of the time when she assumes this attacking posture she doesn't really intend to see the battle through; it's basically a defence mechanism, mostly empty bravado: '*Quietly escaping the counter challenge you've initiated.*'

Leopard

The poet celebrates the countless spots of the leopard, how she attacks prey with surprises and is full of tricks. He mocks her by pointing out that she might even intend to fly into the sky to hunt for food if possible, and that she even goes swimming in order to catch prey (fish). The poet suggests that she can never change her wicked manners: '*Countless rainstorms have often tried… to rub off your spots to no avail.*' Old habits die hard!

Millipede

The poet refers to the millipede as a living train with countless tiny coaches. He describes the roundness of her body and millions of legs, hence her name. Her movement rhythms are captured by the poet: '*In waves and waves*.' Emphasis is placed on her ability to crawl on impossible terrains without tripping, despite her tiny legs. She never takes her bath yet is always clean and shiny. The poet also celebrates her defence mechanism of coiling-up in the face of danger when touched.

Chameleon

The poet sees the chameleon as a '*multi-coloured living wonder of ancient days*.' He comments on how she struggles to walk even the shortest of distances, and that's why she often changes colour, according to the poet; to avoid detection. The poet believes there might be a heavenly oath or bond between her and nature that no one can understand, especially her feeding habit with that awful tongue.

Bat

The poet amuses himself with the funny looks and nature of the bat; she is neither fully here nor there, with queer personality and resemblances: '*My wings like umbrellas; far cry from feathers*.' He is further surprised by the acrobatic stance of the bat and her form of relaxation in the cave that passes as her home.

Cricket

The poet praises the terrible but wonderful shrill of the cricket during the night time. The poet believes it's a meaningful mode of communication in the cricket world, and only they can understand it. But why disturb everyone with it, the poet ponders.

Dolphin

The poet extols the dwelling place of the dolphin, her communication skills, her social contacts and life, her survival tactics in the waters and her relationship with and love for humans, who she refers to as playmates.

Penguin

The poet describes where penguins inhabit on the planet and the temperature of such locations. He describes the shape of the animal, her survival instincts and characteristics, even her preferred food in the wild.

Zebra

The poet lauds the natural beauty of the zebra as the apple of everyone's eye, making it a target. Her life is in the hands of predators in the jungle. She appreciates man's concern about her safety but points out, '*But who can save us from ourselves?*'

Panda

The poet explores the main diet of the panda in the jungle (bamboo leaves) and the location where she can be found on the globe. He further celebrates the beauty of her natural colour blend. The poet also notes that the panda is a territorial animal and never takes it kindly if anyone encroaches on her territory. Her might and defence mechanisms are well celebrated – '*paw-pads, infested with mighty claws*'.

Skunk

The poet hails the individuality of the animal, her survival instincts in the wild and her defence mechanism – '*my foul-smelling liquid*'.

Rhinoceros

The poet describes the shape of the rhino's nose; his thick skin, symbolising toughness and might; his size. The poet celebrates the natural food chains or webs as the rhino allows the egrets to feed off his back, picking up the ticks and body parasites feeding on his own blood. The poet finally celebrates the survival of the fittest mentality that rules in the animal kingdom.

Whale

The poet exalts the mighty nature of the whale as the largest mammal on planet earth. The poet also makes a biblical reference to Jonah in the belly of the whale for three days and nights. He equally celebrates the oils that are the natural gift of the whale to mankind.

Octopus

The poet applauds the wonderful nature of the octopus with her multiple legs as a boneless wonder.

Kangaroo

A celebration of the wonderful nature of the kangaroo as marsupial. The poet refers to her as an '*Australian pride*' and details where she can be found. The poet paints a graphic picture of how she juggles the roles of motherhood, bread-winning and safety in a single breath in the precarious animal kingdom.

Fox

The poet describes the fox as a dog but with a great difference from dogs, referring to her as a great nuisance. The poet mocks the fox for her poor relationship with the chickens – she is an unwelcome visitor in their homes as they see the fox as false.

Rabbit

The rabbit's natural, secret habitat and sense of alertness to danger are espoused and celebrated. Her luck of having large eyes is equally commended.

Part Three

Selected Poems as Comprehension Passages

Attempt the following questions:

Pig

1. What saves the pig from the cold?

2. The pig says 'one must feed'. From where?

3. What is 'like raindrops on umbrellas'?

4. '…not for your wedding…' What is being referred to here?

5. According to the pig, what is his ultimate pleasure?

Goat

1. Who is agile but stupid?

2. What is the goat's favourite pastime?

3. 'Loved by all but hated to bear my name.' What does this refer to?

4. How does the goat compete with men?

5. According to the goat, what often happens in his bitter experience?

Hen, Poultry

1. What is the hen's lot in life?

2. 'Have wings; can barely fly…' Explain this.

3. 'Never stop pecking...' Explain.

4. Who feeds on everything yet without teeth?

5. 'Each passing day; a bonus in the hands of man...' Explain.

Horse, Stallion

1. 'Those rustic times...' What is being referred to here?

2. 'Dragged to the battlefield; their will, not mine...' Explain.

3. How was the horse robbed of every excuse to retreat?

4. What could prompt '...cracked back from unfriendly whips'?

5. 'Would have been long dead and buried...' If not for what?

Cat

1. Who vanishes at unpleasant sounds?

2. What puts rats and birds on edge?

3. 'Don't believe in sharing...' Refers to who?

4. What happens when the cat is disturbed?

5. What could leave an intruder in a sorry case?

6. 'As —— you get the best of me...' Fill in the blank.

Lion

1. Who is being referred to here: '*In utter confidence...*'?

2. '*All scamper for cover...*' Refers to what?

3. '*King of the Jungle...*' Who does this refer to?

4. '*A total deceit...*' Refers to?

5. When does the lion's true self jump out?

Pigeon

1. '*Like a helicopter, as free as the air...*' What does this refer to?

2. '*Apple of every eye.*' Who is being referred to here?

3. What does the pigeon do at the pool in Trafalgar Square?

4. Explain the following: '*With clean hearts, not killing hearts...*'

5. Explain: '*Unity is strength; their United Kingdom.*'

Tortoise

1. Whose appearance shows his manner?

2. Whose folktales tell us about the tortoise?

3. What makes one quake with laughter?

4. What is the tortoise's shell like?

5. What does his shell help the tortoise to hide?

Cow

1. Whose meat serves the needs of man?
2. *'Mountain-like structure…'* What figure of speech is this?
3. What part of the cow sustains our health?
4. Mention four parts of the cow that help man and how.
5. Who, again, does man thank for these?

Monkey

1. Who is a master of the treetops?
2. Quote the line that compares monkey to man. What figure of speech is this?
3. Who is always desperate and without considerations for peers?
4. Quote a line that expresses the funny side of the monkey.
5. According to the poet, what are the three things that make a monkey *'a far cry from decency'*?

Hedgehog

1. How does the poet describe the means of protection of the hedgehog?
2. How does he ward off attacks?
3. Who is glad to have escaped unhurt?
4. *'Coast clear, it uncoils itself…'* Who?
5. What does he do next?

Snake

1. 'Charmers can not be even too sure...' Refers to what?

2. '...Heaven-bound, without special grace to rescue.' What could lead to this?

3. 'Genesis of enmity to mankind...' Explain.

4. How does the snake feed?

5. What does the poet want the snake to accept?

Dog

1. Who shields his Master from dubious intruders?

2. What is the dog's form of communication?

3. What is the first law of his nature?

4. What is the dog's stock-in-trade, according to the poet?

5. What is the dog's favourite pastime?

Elephant

1. Who is Hercules of the jungle, according to the writer?

2. 'Legs like tree-trunks...' What figure of speech is this?

3. Identify other similes within the poem.

4. The writer expresses surprises – what are they?

5. 'Tusks; a sweet-bitter gift of nature.' Explain.

Giraffe

1. What leaves a designer green with envy?

2. 'Like gossips...' Refers to?

3. According to the writer, what 'makes a spy green with envy'?

4. What does one never stops to wonder – according to the poet?

5. 'Olympic gold standard...' What does the poet refer to?

Ostrich

1. To an ostrich, what's an after-thought?

2. Who is the queen of birds?

3. Explain: 'Naked from neck to head...'

4. Explain: 'Burying head in sand...'

5. 'Oh, incomprehensible folly/wisdom, you know better...' What does the poet mean by the underlined words?

Parrot

1. Who is a word-leaker, according to the poet?

2. Explain 'open secrets' according to the poet.

3. Where are parrots usually kept at home?

4. Why is Master always cautious when his parrot is around?

5. 'Spill the beans...' Explain what the poet means.

Bull vs. Fighter

1. What is a taboo to the bulls?

2. Who is 'costumed', according to the poet?

3. 'Life and death game...' Explain.

4. 'Either must taste the bitter pill of death...' Explain.

Camel

1. The poet refers to the camel as what?

2. Who is the 'Lord of the desert'?

3. 'With heaven and earth...' Refers to?

4. 'Incomparable'. What does the poet refer to?

5. 'Must go on knees for Master to climb aback...' Refers to?

Grizzly Bear

1. Who has 'claw-infested toes', according to the poet?

2. How does the writer describe the might of a bear?

3. What is engaged in countless styles?

4. What does the bear feed on, according to the poet?

5. What does the bear's face look like?

Scorpion

1. 'A sting; bucketful of tears...' The writer refers to?

2. 'Everyone's a suspect...' Explain.

3. 'Come not near and nurse no regrets.' Explain.

4. What happens in the line 'With eyes full of tears'?

5. What does the scorpion's baby do on its back? Explain.

Cockroach

1. Where are the places the cockroach says he'll be waiting?

2. What could be his size?

3. Why does she wear your shoes out of your sight?

4. What does she say she's not scared of?

Spider

1. '...How I enjoy those spots...' Explain.

2. 'My complex mansions...' Refers to?

3. What advantage does the spider's home have?

4. According to the spider, 'A wonder to many...' What is this a reference to?

5. What does the spider refer to as 'child's play'?

Housefly

1. Who comes around to say hi?

2. How does the fly claim to help observe prayers?

3. How does he claim to show friendship?

4. '*Giving a dog a bad name…*' What is referred to here?

5. '*Soon going to get immune to those…*' What does this mean?

Mosquito

1. '*Naughty vampire…*' Refers to what?

2. Why does the mosquito steal in '*like a thief in the night*'?

3. '*Which makes me risk this single life.*' What's being referred to here?

4. What leaves one at the mercy of our Lord, according to the mosquito?

5. According to the mosquito, what does man do to him when he really wants to be cruel?

Bee

1. '*Hours on end in my field.*' What is being referred to here?

2. '*That golden juice…*' Refers to?

3. Who does the bee refers to in the line *'Lazy man in his idleness'*?

4. *'All my savings robbed overnight…'* What savings?

5. According to the bee, *'the fruits of my toil'* refers to what?

Ant vs. Grasshopper

1. *'Never allows a minute's rest…'* This refers to?

2. *'Your curse like rain on an umbrella…'* What does this mean?

3. *'Make haste while the sun shines.'* What does this mean?

4. *'Who else if not me?'* Who said this?

5. Whose laughter comes last?

Snail

1. What is being dragged *'all day'*?

2. What is the writer's view of the function of the liquids in the snail?

3. What does the snail do when conditions become tough?

4. *'What a burden…'* What is the writer referring to here?

5. *'Bound of flesh…'* Refers to?

Crab

1. Where do crabs live?

2. '*Six-legged; with scissors-like claws…*' Refers to?

3. Describe the crab's movement.

4. '*Dot-like eyes that pick you out like a satellite…*' What figure of speech is this?

5. Where can a crab's bag be found?

Praying Mantis

1. In *Praying Mantis*, the '*countless pins*' are located where?

2. What is the usefulness of its hind legs?

3. Who dares all in emergency bouts?

4. What is the complexion of the praying mantis?

Leopard

1. What is the leopard's daily bread?

2. Whose surprise visits leads to demise?

3. Who is referred to here as '*bag of tricks*'?

4. How could birds' lives be endangered?

5. According to the poet, '*countless rainstorms*' couldn't do what?

Millipede

1. Who is a living train with tiny coaches?
2. 'All moving in waves and waves.' What is referred to here?
3. 'Passing through thick and thin…' Explain.
4. What is the 'marvel of nature', according to the poet?
5. What does the millipede do at the touch of an enemy?

Chameleon

1. Who is referred to as 'Multi-coloured living wonder of ancient days'? Explain.
2. 'Struggling to walk, like an old man…' What figure of speech is this?
3. Why does the chameleon change colours, according to the poet?
4. What is an oath, according to the poet?
5. What does the chameleon use to capture prey?

Bat

1. Whose wings are like an umbrella?
2. 'Wings like umbrellas…' What figure of speech is this?
3. Do bats have feathers?
4. How does the bat perch on twigs?
5. Where do bats live?

Cricket

1. 'Silent in the day, vibrant at night...' Refers to?

2. 'Shrill upon shrill...' Refers to?

3. 'Disorganising the rational thought of men.' Refers to?

4. The poet refers to these noises as what?

5. 'Thickness of the blackness of the darkness...' What figure of speech is this?

Rhinoceros

1. The stump on the nose of the rhino is likened to what by the poet?

2. What feeds on the back of the rhino?

3. What sucks the rhino's blood?

4. 'A web that links all living... none are spared the agony...' What agony is being referred to here by the poet?

5. According to the rhino, 'Tomorrow is not promised to anyone.' What does this refer to?

Whale

1. What is the largest mammal off shore?

2. According to the poet, who is a celebrity compared to others?

3. According to the poet, what's like a stadium?

4. What is referred to as the whale's token of appreciation for nature's goodness?

5. What figures of speech are the following:

'*wild, wide world…*'

'*dead, dark depth…*'

Octopus

1. How many legs does the octopus have?

2. Why does he squirt black ink?

3. Where could suction cups be found on the octopus?

4. Why is the octopus flexible, according to the writer?

5. How many eyes does it have?

Kangaroo

1. What is a pouch?

2. Where can a kangaroo be found?

3. What is its baby called?

4. How does it move?

5. What does the poet liken the kangaroo's head to?

Part Four
Fun and Games

Animal Kingdom Search Game and Others

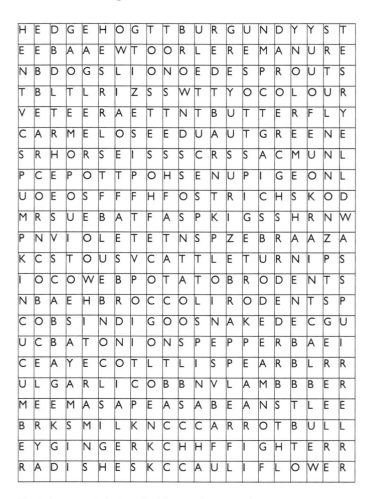

H	E	D	G	E	H	O	G	T	T	B	U	R	G	U	N	D	Y	Y	S	T
E	E	B	A	A	E	W	T	O	O	R	L	E	R	E	M	A	N	U	R	E
N	B	D	O	G	S	L	I	O	N	O	E	D	E	S	P	R	O	U	T	S
T	B	L	T	L	R	I	Z	S	S	W	T	T	Y	O	C	O	L	O	U	R
V	E	T	E	E	R	A	E	T	T	N	T	B	U	T	T	E	R	F	L	Y
C	A	R	M	E	L	O	S	E	E	D	U	A	U	T	G	R	E	E	N	E
S	R	H	O	R	S	E	I	S	S	S	C	R	S	S	A	C	M	U	N	L
P	C	E	P	O	T	T	P	O	H	S	E	N	U	P	I	G	E	O	N	L
U	O	E	O	S	F	F	F	H	F	O	S	T	R	I	C	H	S	K	O	D
M	R	S	U	E	B	A	T	F	A	S	P	K	I	G	S	S	H	R	N	W
P	N	V	I	O	L	E	T	E	T	N	S	P	Z	E	B	R	A	A	Z	A
K	C	S	T	O	U	S	V	C	A	T	T	L	E	T	U	R	N	I	P	S
I	O	C	O	W	E	B	P	O	T	A	T	O	B	R	O	D	E	N	T	S
N	B	A	E	H	B	R	O	C	C	O	L	I	R	O	D	E	N	T	S	P
C	O	B	S	I	N	D	I	G	O	O	S	N	A	K	E	D	E	C	G	U
U	C	B	A	T	O	N	I	O	N	S	P	E	P	P	E	R	B	A	E	I
C	E	A	Y	E	C	O	T	L	T	L	I	S	P	E	A	R	B	L	R	R
U	L	G	A	R	L	I	C	O	B	B	N	V	L	A	M	B	B	B	E	R
M	E	E	M	A	S	A	P	E	A	S	A	B	E	A	N	S	T	L	E	E
B	R	K	S	M	I	L	K	N	C	C	C	A	R	R	O	T	B	U	L	L
E	Y	G	I	N	G	E	R	K	C	H	H	F	F	I	G	H	T	E	R	R
R	A	D	I	S	H	E	S	K	C	C	A	U	L	I	F	L	O	W	E	R

Find the words below hidden in the grid above.

Animals:

EAGLE, CATS, DOGS, HORSES, GOAT, PIG, BAT, LAMB, HEN, COW, HEDGEHOG, MOSQUITO, BEAR, BEE, BULL, GRASSHOPPERS, ANT, OWL, SNAKE, RODEO, ZEBRA, OSTRICH, TIGER, BUTTERFLY, RODENT, CAMEL, SQUIRREL, PARROT.

Colours:

GREEN, YELLOW, BURGUNDY, INDIGO, BROWN, GOLDEN, ORANGE, COLOUR.

Farm Produce & Vegetables:

PEAR, ONIONS, YAM, POTATO, PUMPKIN, BEANS, PEAS, MESH, GINGER, RADISHES, CARROTS, TURNIPS, CABBAGE, CORN COBS, CELERY, OKRA, CAULIFLOWER, LETTUCE, PEPPER, BROCCOLI, SPROUTS, MILK, MANURE, BARN, APPLE.

Animal Kingdom Code Game

A	B	C	D	E	F	G	H	I	J	K	L	M	N	O
1	2	3	4	5	6	7	8	9	10	11	12	13	14	15
P	Q	R	S	T	U	V	W	X	Y	Z				
16	17	18	19	20	21	22	23	24	25	26				

In the grid above each letter of the alphabet has been given a number. Crack the following codes using the grid:

1. 16,9,7; 9,19; 4,9,18,20,25; 1,14,9,13,1,12

2. 13,25,14,15,19,5; 18,9,14,7; 14,15,20; 6,15,18; 25,15,21,18; 23,5,5,4,9,14,7; 18,8,14,7,9.

3. 26,15,15;9,19;23,8,5,18,5; 1,14, 9,13,1,12,19; 11,5,5,16,20.

4. 16,9,7,5,15,14,19; 8,15,22,5,18,19; 9,14; 20,8,5; 19,11,25; 12,9,11,5; 8,5,12,93,15,22,5; 1,4,9,13,1,12; 11,9,147,4,15,13; 16,15,5,13,19.

5. 9; 12,15,22,5; 1.14,9,13,1,12; 11,9,47,4,15 13; 16,15,5,13,19.

Now turn the following into code:

6. Lions often look for someone to devour

7. Cow's milk and its meat sustain our health

22441072R00067

Printed in Great Britain
by Amazon